The Lyrics

Other Books by Fanny Howe

The Lyrics

FANNY HOWE

Graywolf Press
SAINT PAUL, MINNESOTA

Publication of this volume is made possible in part by a grant provided by the Minnesota State Arts Board, through an appropriation by the Minnesota State Legislature; a grant from the Wells Fargo Foundation Minnesota; and a grant from the National Endowment for the Arts, which believes that a great nation deserves great art. Significant support has also been provided by the Bush Foundation; Target; the McKnight Foundation; and other generous contributions from foundations, corporations, and individuals. To these organizations and individuals we offer our heartfelt thanks.

MINNESOTA
STATE ARTS BOARD

NATIONAL
ENDOWMENT
FOR THE ARTS

TARGET.

Published by Graywolf Press
2402 University Avenue, Suite 203
Saint Paul, Minnesota 55114
All rights reserved.

www.graywolfpress.org

Published in the United States of America

ISBN 978-1-55597-472-5

2 4 6 8 9 7 5 3 1
First Graywolf Printing, 2007

Library of Congress Control Number: 2006938266

Cover design: Kyle G. Hunter

Cover art: Italo Scanga, "Counter-Reformation Figure"

To Patrick

Acknowledgments

First I want to thank the Bellagio Foundation, the Guggenheim Foundation, Kenyon College, the Lannan Foundation (Marfa), the editors at Graywolf, and the monks at Glenstal Abbey for providing me with the means to write these poems. And I want to extend unending gratitude to the editors of magazines who are committed to poetry and who published some of the poems in this collection. These include *American Letters and Commentary, Arson, Brick*, the *Canary*, the *Chicago Review, Columbia Review, Elizabeth Street, Five Fingers Review, Golden Handcuffs Review, LIT, Lyric, Ploughshares, Poker, Vallum* (in a chapbook called "Tramp"), Artery Editions (on a CD and in a folder called *Spiral*), and *Xantippe*. If I have forgotten someone, or printed a revised version in two different places, I apologize and chalk it up to itinerant living.

Contents

Forty Days

1.

It's the summer solstice
The day the darkening begins

If I keep walking west
I can precede this time again

In a year. Not much stamina
Foot-shoes sore

Passing war after war
Between ad-nauseum errors

Unsure of which was after
And which is before

If I can just keep walking
It will not be now
But next

If I can stay with the gravity
That troubles the sea you'll see
I will come to that day

Now I can taste its goodness
Without me

After the solstice
Has passed, the days contract
New green grays
And I'm off again

To those I would die for
Please be patient
It's summer somewhere
I hear good things

The ferry holds fast
To the sound it makes
A rumble, a whistle
Half-white raindrops
Racing and at war
Glass that bristles
And wrinkles at the sill
Children finger the window
And blow
Each one, all ones
Already away

When I walk by myself
I often hit a river
With no water in it—black lyric
Undertow to preordained ethics

A template and a mirror
Of unmined silver

There some gems tear at their colors all night

Particles of petrified spirit
Live inside this matter

Peters and Pauls
"Known only to God"

Double the beautiful
Because they are so little

A potato field whitens in the sun
And someone rushes in
Passing roses, fuschia and orange
Four-petaled flowers

The sky is a piece of the painting
Placed on a wall outside

Into your arms she runs, lost one,
Whenever she hears you crying

Veer uninvited
Veer towards the winding river

Low bridge and parchment sky

Uninvited veer
Back the way

You came here. To follow
The unhosted highway

2.

Where, if I go far enough, will I find a sacred place?

On the terraced gardens of the Barrington estate?
The family left when their daughter was shot by the IRA.

Now a Bible garden is here—myrrh, Judas Tree, artichokes,
marjoram that blows from bed to bed, all the spices from the
Bible, extra horse flies that bite, and a huge tumbling fig tree.

I am among the Benedictines again.

The sun and St. John's Wort
Produce the fragrance of a candle burning inside a
    honeycomb.

The monks will cook and offer me food from childhood:
Mashed potatoes with grilled tomatoes
Blackened haddock, boiled potatoes,
Overcooked string beans, peas,
Curried chicken, rice,
Soup made from potatoes and vegetable of the day before.
Green soup.
Rice pudding with bitter hot applesauce,
Brown bread, butter and black currant jam,
Gooseberry and marmalade,
Sausages and black pudding.

The nights are damp and cold, I am sleepless still.
Yet missed Matins.
And drank tea with more milk than usual.
Brothers Malachy, Ciaran, Patrick, Terence, Simon,
Then Berna, Alice, Sue and me convene in the meditation
    room.

In The Rule it says: "The Abbess should always remember
What she is and what she is called.
Let her understand also
What a difficult and arduous task she has undertaken:
Ruling souls and adapting herself to a variety of characters."

Now the bees are coming in the window from the yellow
    flowers that are like mallow.

Ciaran and I took a long walk in the summer sun.
Tennis courts, meadows, woods and ducking under electrified
wires to get to the rust brown lake. One dreams into a book
a day like this, made of grass and nothing else. At supper
tonight he played the Goldberg Variations that I bought for
him while his brothers ate chicken croquettes in silence.

Yogananda believes that the Word is consciousness, it is a
    seed implanted in the person.
A word is a vibratory presence.

I think a sentence is a long word.

Are words to sentences what letters are to words?
What have I been doing all these years?

Why does this matter unless it reveals something about the
    structure of the universe?

Bread and drink and soup are the staples here.
Still, the Irish brought potatoes to Idaho.

In the library Brother Cyprian, the organist, explains my
poems to me perfectly. He is the one who wrote: "The
improviser spins his metaphysic of utopia, presses the whole
liturgy, rite and participants in one, towards the future."

Cosmic vibrations tremble the sanctuary's green cloth over the host. A red candle is burning across an oriental rug, there is an animal Irish-Celtic design on the altar: I know that the best thing for others might be happening because I am not there.

As in cut, pare, prune, reduce, mine.

Still, pills to sleep before I'm gone.

3.

What is shorter than a step?
An indrawn breath.
Not remembered when done
Not when not done either.

It's the animal soul.
The Great Spirit who lolls
As time and broods.

During cemetery strolls
Breath comes and goes
Unnoticed. Melancholy is
Disavowed, no time for tone.

Plum buds have bloomed
On lilac Sunday in early May.
City property is sanctified
By pedestrian traffic.

What is heavier than lead?
Cries that can't be heard.
Brother Granite.

4.

Orange lilies are freckled brown,
Both seed and paper rotting,

But there is a weary sub-zone
At the level of wood.

The principle is understood
To be failure at a certain level, dreadful

Numbness hitting
Just when the sun penetrates the hill
Like a squint before a squadron.

Then someone welcomes the mother's return
As a virgin.

5.

Today is the Feast of the Lost Season.
Ripe fruits are hoarded
In the temple and painted over.
People are grabbing and complaining.

Wine and plump breads, pagan
Images to the lurid father-god
Are up for sale and
Shrunk by the imagination.

In the old days
Hell came through experience
Paradise through the eyes
But long predatory Purgatory
Was always the true story of working lives.

Now I lay me down
As a minor contribution to the great machine.

6.

Lost won't admit she's lonely or it's late.
Cellophane leaves
Orange on the school windowpanes.
Children's things are stuck on everything.
Say it, they're divine. Go outside.
Tear down the crucifix.
Stop the folk stories. Peppermills
And girls sacrificed for gold.
Nail up the sacred heart.
You've got to start walking again
As what you have become
Since childhood put you in relation
To star, road, rotation.

7.

Was in the month of Mary
That I lost my desire to pray.
It seeped away like yellow
Until it was as blurred as sorrow.
It was me passing on my hope to a solo:
God became weak and subtle.
Birdsong was my last communion:
The chirp of karma, the caw of eros,
Piercing delirium, the laugh of the futile,
A sacred heart with wings,
Fruit of the whistle,
The lyrics of the sparrow.

8.

When donkeys traveled
Without glancing to the side,
Long-lashed and buckled
Inside their own hide,
When they brayed for joy
Into the gray industrial clouds
And the cows replied
Like balloons deflating into moos,
The strain on the immaculate heart
Was as grave as it could get.
Awful pity.
To be so blessed
As to pound for happiness.

9.

Near a bombed post office
In a kind of Dublin
The rain began autumn
And a day. All fell flat
On the cracks, the rest
Was dry from draining
While walls were axed
By the torrential pain.
The sacred heart was here
Observed for study.
Things mean things.
Not just in books one looks,
One pries and one is ignorant—
But also in the reader's mind.

10.

I tasted the Word and it wasn't bitter
Until it reached my solar plexus.
Then its letters grew thin as wires.
Tincture of benzedrine.
The deep red stain of iodine.
Like Mastroianni's smile—
Its seductive irony
That I must adore or die.

Sweet as religion
Without ethics
An emptying mind on the road, no more crucifix
Or dogma. An electromagnetic altar.

11.

Before the star bowl tips
And I can fall without fear,
How will I support a bed,
A candle, the chilly sheets, the thoughts of a planet
Girdled by rust?

I've been twelve winters
In this auxillary star-drome,
Spaces dominated by ice.
Heat-resisting contacts, chilled to shrivel.
Like diamond mines spanked
On the bosoms of the idle
And the sparkle of sweat in the creases of the rest.

This is such an old story, listen.
The poor are hard-working
And the rich get more through talking.
Money has always
Been huge and out of sight like God
Who does not exist but is.

Yes, you, the lip of the cosmos, its cervix
Way out, silver and flat,
You the sun revolving around us
Earthself caught, parsed and drowned
Leaving every wall the color of a shadow
Smoke in the seats, second class
Ourselves in transition
While the wind blew east across the globe
And into the eye of the gun.

My children lay back on a blue seat
The train window their first film

Stains speeding past without moving, their eyes
Blurring at the confusion
Between outside and on.

There's one piece of knowledge, if I don't have it,
How will I get by, go forward, get on
Where will the hope come from
How will I pay
For morphine, swill, phenobarbitol,
The bag for my head, the applesauce, the ticket
To the forest to get lost in, the ice floe to ride on,
The typhoon, the ledge, the will to starve?

12.

Give me my shawl, my corkscrew
And my cloth bag.
Give me my hot water bottle and my book.
Give me my stick and my water.
One shoe for walking and one to dance.
No stability. Thirst.
The will to keep moving.
An instrument's heat.
Bald mountains and a spider that was a leaf.
The scheme is organic, it knows itself.
See that light across the enslaved sea?
Redemption time knows when.

13.

If I were Jesus, would you slap both sides of my face?
If I were Jesus, would you stamp on my hands?
If I was Jesus, would you lock me up?
Would you make me crawl down the prison hall?
Would you cover my head?
Stick my face in the pot? Would you rape me?
If I were Jesus, would you break down the door?
Would you wreck the house and terrify my family?
If I was Jesus, would you bomb my trees, my place
Of parables, the fig trees and the rivers of wheat?
If I were Jesus—

Well, I'm not. So please—Go right ahead.

14.

I was a ghost before I was a tramp.
I crossed into a landscape
      Where everything was finished.
Fallen branches, the city dump,
      This was the past on which my ghost stepped.

What had happened there
      Was the foundation of here.
      It was the finished text
Across which I moved, and everyone else beside me.

I was the ghost of someone
      Who dissolved into spirit-parts
      First when she gave birth.
(Reproduction meant she was always elsewhere
      With another name.)

Then later no days or acts were separate
      And the word "one" was an extra word.

The rest would follow,
A continuum of ones.

15.

Like a night prayer as black as the Bible
Gold-leaved pages
With no words on them
A new blend of material
Ink white and draining
Layer to layer
And pages because there is paper

And paper because there was prayer
Or night fear. That is, an idea.

You have lines linking stars to stars
In ourselves our cosmos, the illusion
Of nothing between them an error
Because you are a mirror.

16.

Hell changed its plans
And came in the middle
Instead of the end.
This was a good thing
For the burning of karma.
I lay down my life
First for the third time,
Then not the second
But finally ready
To embrace layers all at once.
Fever for medicine
The parting of layers never.

17.

In the perfumery, you can have a shot of tea among
as many grays as there are levels, and under a huge wedge
    tomb on a hill.

Mild sun into evening.
Makuru, carrying fire from one camp to the next, like dreams.

In Milltown Malbay, trad music in a pub, a windy night, pale pink fuchsia fluttering, clouds of different densities layer under the near-full moon

Being between-things, I thought about improvisation and Simone Weil's *metaxu*.

An old desolate hotel on the beach was facing west to America, rocky but flat and a banner flapping. Summer bungalows for lease.

Where are the little people of Ireland?
They are the elfin Santas at Shannon Airport. Robots with realistic hideous faces.

Is this what was carried from the megalithic household ring, the laborious stones. Shapes primordial from dull comprehension, each circle and wedge resulting in lots of muscle pain?

A plastic ice cream cone with a whirling white spiral stands on village corners. looks delicious and archetypal.

A ring fort wall, the elderberry bush, might offer shelter for kid goats and lambs, like an imagined fairy pen.

18.

Because my secret wedding
Was enduring and the rest
Was not—I think disclosure
Is dangerous.

What is heavier than lead?
The need for bread.

What is crueler than a boss?
The need for praise.
What is shorter than a step?
An indrawn breath.

My secret wedding was to whom?
A promise not a human.

19.

Rice was the price of happiness,
Just a spray of it that stuck to the man's purse.
Glass doesn't form drops or circles when it breaks.
But water does. He doesn't want water or glass.
What does this signify?

It is an example surely.
Have you forgotten what a thing represents
In waking life?
The lantern in a human brain colorizes the green
In a grain of rice. The woman who takes rice
In exchange for happiness
Is called avaricious because happiness
Is free in certain places.

20.

Three bells in a long garden

Two eyes in a baby's head

One route to arrival

Via hope's will.
One might lie flat
One might lie still.
One might bang rocks

In the mighty hills.

Echo, Sir Echo

Where's my true love?

Echo, Sir Echo
Where's my true love?

21.

The sky, my loom, is under me.
My foot rests on air.

It's in my hair
The wind is weaving.

Clack and pedal.
Propeller and reactor.

My garden droops
With bleeding heart.

Thick oily leaves.
Brick and buttresses.

Abstract berries.
Spikes and watching lights.

Down here is the worker zone.
Over there is management.

22.

The partisans resisted. They formed
Collectives under the pines.
Communal acts, collective results.
Continuing revolution.

They lived in forests and died
Because insurgence meant
You were going to be killed.

Cook first, kill later.
Hot wood, hot water.

No struggle can depend
On individual survival.
You should have seen
The spontaneity required!

23.

Hey, afraid
The disenfranchised
Made the first machines of labor?
So to build prisons
Around themselves?

What if the man said "walking stick"
Instead of "get to work"?
What if he said "You are your own
Trap and lock"?

Afraid the rape bed
Was comfy?
No pleasure, no me?

Stop at the little beehive
Behind that tree.

24.

Five-starred flowers
Whitened their scents.
They knew that certain fragrances
Are the same as shapes.
They knew they were white,
Having studied gaudy nights
By the lakefront,
Black Moroccan grapes
And Persian windmills.
A seed can be stamped on
And still want to live.
The scheme hates lack.
Zion and Sinai are not the same place.
Words know that.

25.

Let the mill-clapper go on clacking,

Let mud and ink stiffen
On the same sheet.

Let the lamb shit on the cross
And the pen cut the butcher.

Let a fire blow and warm
The revolutionaries.

I am secular. I walk the streets.
I feel sorry for everyone.

When will the Messiah come?
The repetition of the same problem

Is getting exhausting.
"Roosters, blood, a silhouette.
Hanging over a gas lamp."

26.

If you don't see it at night, where is it?
Permeated by forgetfulness, an eternity of Z's.
The gas of consciousness
Stays gentle and without influence
Its end-pinnings dropped. Spaces between synapses
Enlarge to let in light.
A chemical air that is non-odorific
Thinning walls from excess use.
My sight fell short was its flaw
Not a mistake but a misreading of distances
In order to stay free.

27.

Miranda,
Manna tastes of your wish
To taste it.
Taste your wish, not yeast

Or fruit.
Manna is white and soft.

What was that island we were on?
If it wasn't a vision
But an actual place
Who was that stranger beside us?
Please forgive me for insisting
It must have been a dream.
No one could survive such happiness.

28.

A day is a freely given poem; it can be short or long.
Contradiction, coincidence.

An emotional experience.
Perseverance through hell.

A series of events you must not forget.
Twelve sunsets, twenty nine dawns, all in one.

An epiphany.
How long your hopes last

Until the next poem.

29.

Call out.
Press nine.

I will hear some shift of gray in the air.
Will ingest the frost of its silence.

A six-foot bed
And a sprawler's sigh through the wall

Of this fifty-pound hotel
Occupied by the dropped.

Call out, no call back.

Fall fast forward without will
To the window.

The other world is pressed
Against the glass:

A kind of heaven, a known nothing.

Call out to the cone-opening light
To colors never seen before

But most familiar.

Call out of the grit in your tissue
Before your days are written

Or you will be too late for the answer.

Be really primitive.
A thin finger picture

Of nature undernurtured.

Like egg, parchment, glue and the breath of the artist.

Call come in at last
Immaterial

When or where
A message from *that*.

I will be packed into people
Against a strange tin.

Vehicles will glitter
And polyphony the interrupter

Will cut every sentence in half.

Call I won't call back.
Call up into the night:

"Knower, how is this voice different from the others?"

School

1.

Paper is twisted
in the thin green trees

It's daybreak

A furry cloud huddles
on the groundswell

Light bulbs yellow
and shrill bells ring

School time!

2.

Lengthening attention
to the tar-black
roof

ends with the glitter
of mica and ice

Books won't help a child
get out of this
house without pity

3.

White plaster
and desks turned over

Schoolteachers' faces
made of brick

If she hurts her
and she hurts her

and if he hates him
and he hates him

then she might hit him
whom he hates

by mistake

4.

In one child's idea
of paradise

there is no person
but parchment

paper and a thumb-sized sun

like a blinking crown
from a broken crayon

5.

Miles measured

from here to home
by breath

Distance from
and between

doors
enlarging still more to come

to those who break the rules

but which one angrily
which one for fun?

6.

School is a city
like Providence

It is usually distant

Sometimes you can mistake it
for fate

or sometimes coincidence

because it re-emerges
after you have passed its gates

Gray blocks penciled on a dull sky
or a dull sky penciled onto gray

7.

A child's hair is wilder than a brush
when he/she sits behind a desk

picking at pencils, fighting
to stamp down anguish

and keep it low on static

Already he/she is learning
that in life

the meanest are winning

like illness fighting to survive
or illness wanting to live

under the name of Necessity

8.

No whistling or shitting
No whispering, no smiling
No kissing or pinching
allowed in this place

No dogs or cats
No traps or nets
No bullets, no arrows
No nail files, no glass

No trust in the place
is allowed in this place
No critiques of the teacher
No teacher without a hitch

No cheating on answers
No flying, no dropping

No drinks or food
are allowed in this place

No climbing down
under the desk; no looking out
at infinity; it's temporary
No music, no dance

No joking, no shouts
A house without chaos
is what we have planned
Adjust!!

9.

Shrill bells ring

Light bulbs yellow
Run like hell

A furry cloud huddles
on the groundswell

It's dusk at three
and paper flutters

in the thin black trees

School's out!

City Limits

1.

Rain and a splash
    of backward glances from horses
    climbing out of the river.

They are factored out of all equations,
    the luckies. Their shoes
    ring like elfin hammers

and echo on the granite.

2.

From the yellow mist she came to the hospital
    bruised all over and the man asking
Who did this to you?

But now I don't recall
    what she answered.

The more you lie, the less you remember.
Her plan is not to become a ghost at any cost.

A female ghost is at the bottom of the barrel.
So what's to blame
    except the horse in the sun.

3.

The battlefield is where
bombs are planted in a trash can
roosters are crowing

and ink is like mud.
A chicken lives in the kitchen.

That gas lamp provides a silhouette.
History, there are no surprises coming from you.
From bodies, less than none.

Less than none means there is meaning.

4.

Even among bags, needles and bed pans

Raindrops make ornaments
        out of the lights that shine in them.

Old human breath and an animal soul
        lie down on those horse-hair pillows.

5.

The worst was saved for the best.

The worst was served to the children of the non-avaricious.
A black tomb
of family life, body parts for sale and no sympathy at all.

How can this be happening?
Averted face, a grin.

And these were kind men to everyone at home.

Women loved them.

6.

Horses have fallen on horses
And a heap of laughing soldiers.

No more drama of sulkiness.

They are humans and horses together, they are one thing.

Genesis foot-tap, first out of the yard,
once wrongly placed, the rest
of the hooves follow.

And the pricks
in their pants under massive horse-brown tables
draw up the plans

for continuing slaughter.

7.

"The dragon represents history."

I am running from
these lessons. I am running from school.

Will a new mistake produce better results?

Say I experience once again.
lips on my nipple and the rush
of grief turned into milk. Those
were the days when I understood
emotion as flesh's feelings.

I felt other people more than I knew them.
There were no vapors, even words
stank of milk and mouth.
Love was like a horse. Once I rose
from the bed and left the earth
and my nursing baby and flew
into the likeness of heaven.
But then I volunteered to come back.
Yes, I was a brave soldier then.
I remember baby's eyes were closed
and the sky never looked so smart.
Say I had never had this happen.
Where would I be today?

8.

The horses' flanks are shiny.
They are ears even as they are meat.
They listen to the music
of human voices and leaves and twitch.

Sodomize them, the crowd of bodies cries.
Call on the diligence of the penis
and carnal clitoris, cry the rest.
In music there is rest.

Why did God leave us, isn't it obvious?

Of meaty flanks I sing.
I will go down with the polis.

Let the police drag me away.

"Get rid of those tickets,
Go to the show."

I knew everything was backwards
I didn't need to be told
you were out there, God, or hear
all those cafeteria sounds
in the light that I am,
turning around on a pencil.

9.

Teacher leaned forward and amended
my story about the yellow horse
at the bottom of the road
facing up to where I stood
and coated in silver fog.
He said there was never any fog
in that part of town and I said nothing
though I was the one who went there.

Far and Away

1.

Nobody knows the trouble we saw.
Only the one who caused it.
We were blasted from unified form
Into four clinging to the littlest one.

The worried look. Was it from a memory
Or dread of the future?
All my children facing blue faith
From inside a ruined household.

"Put poison on your leg
To kill the dog
Who bites you," we were advised.
She must have meant spider.

In the basement our teacher
Was swallowed by the stairs
Shadowed by his own head.
Climbing to get us.

He thought he was a watchtower
Light revolving around
His private prison yard.
Both guard and solitary.

In the dots of a corrupted light
In the kind that looks like dust
He and his formed a substance.
You can pass through

"But please leave a residue
For the police . . ."
Talk about soul. You can't dissolve
When you are still standing.

He believed to be righteous
Would bust a crack in this dusk
And he could cut our brains
Into our startled faces.

We would never go home
Again. You'd need a science
To name this new species
That survives without language.

2.

He dreamed I was climbing out on a ledge.
He called for me to stop and come back.
I was disobedient and fell.
So he lost me and I lost everything.

Now there are white flowers in December.
The windows into the worm are open.

If he hadn't called out, he would be exposed.
If he hadn't seen, he would be excused.

A fall is inconsequential.
Malice leaves a mark.

I couldn't have known. I didn't bother to know.
I didn't want to know. Units of music and gin.

Evil is really a weakness in the building's structure.
Way beyond hearing, an act of collapse
Must have a cause
Even in another's dream.

3.

The insane asylum
Was my teacher's mind.

(You can learn who you are from anyone.)

By hand
By fingers cuffed around
A sleeve, he would be tugged away
With pathetic cries
And laughter at others' failures.
Pills, alcohol, more shots
To cure the doses of the nights before.

Everyone I know who lived in Japan
Returned with a Japanese face.

I followed him into his mind.
It was as cold as violet ice cream
In a silver dish.
I choked, and came alive, in that place.

4.

Shake down the whips of white snow
And twilight will be bluer.
Do everything for your eyes,
By your eyes,
And the rest of your body,

Lonely walk to ghostliness.

I loved a long gray liar.
Every hair on his torso.

He was cruel and he smelled of glue.
He was hilarious
And tender-hearted. I was stuck
In a sick fog. A patient and a nurse.

At the time I noted all his flaws.
Now I ask: so what?

5.

There's a long pause when a woman and man
Struggle with equal strength.

A winding road and thick twigged trees
Imitate the palms of two hands.

You, you!

The man dragged me through the streets
I was that insane.

Then he dropped me and the children at a station
Like statues he had cut, baked and broken

Until our ghosts were showing. We tasted rust
While clouds dried in a freshwater sky.

6.

I think it's cold for the Christ
At the final fountain
In a temple of absolute ice
Turquoise and white
All its words and religious music removed to us on paper

This is how transition can be cunning
And belief grows pale and abstract
Until the people crawl
To each other yearning and calling *Teacher!*

His trench coat was just a trench coat.
Now cigarette grit litters the sill
Like blood on a carpet
That refers to a mad minute.
I'm sorry I'm scared of people
When the cloth
Of which they and I are made
Is too tight to switch.

7.

A bird will bite its baby
If it has been touched by an American.
Brittle tweak into the nestling
As soft as seedless jam.
Like that ghost gray arm inside my purse.
Billboards dancing with dew.
Lips crowned with thorns.
Tormented honey tongue
Destruction by addiction.
The health of the brain gone.
Is this a representation or a being?
He only stole when I was looking.
Then the genius hopped like a spark.

8.

There is a ghost on Mary's lap.
His hands drop down because he's at the end.

His coat is open
And his heart-side is pressed against her beating womb.

This is the hour when
She turns into a nurse

Explaining why she has to be a siren first.

Cherry red lights
Hail down on where the men in white coats kneel.

Too late, nihilistic humanity.

Nightlight is evening out over a school yard.
Red petals stick to the blinking asphalt.

(for John Wieners)

9.

Cement in a city park in May
With your stand-in the cherry

Blossoms smeared creamily
Across his knees.

I even loved each hair.

A violin is the opposite of a horse.
Music is made of quarter notes.

I reached up and shook the tree
And the petals floated to the page.

They advised me: *Go home.*
What is sin but distance from the interior.

10.

The city is a desert with water on every side
And strong working people
Pushing along.
Soon I will be one of them.
X forgave Peter three times three
Then went into a nearby garden to cry.
A rejected gesture turns to syrup.
It has a sickening taste
And its color is maroon.
It is a substance you carry around like an island.
I told you love produces more love
Until it is marooned in its own dark hands.
Then it knows something.

11.

In the Book good means glad
And equal means one and one are the same.
It sounds like we should want
To stand up and laugh
All in a row and work
For one thing: another laugh.
Monks ran through a desert
On burning feet.
Not even one day could they last
In the face of the strange. God
Granted me babies who seemed alien
Until they smiled at what I seemed.

12.

The rain falls on.
Acres of violets unfold.
Dandelion, mayflower
Myrtle and forsythia follow.

The cardinals call to each other.
Echoes of delicate
Breath-broken whistles.

I know something now
About subject, object, verb
And about one word that fails
For lack of substance.

Now people say, *He passed on*
Instead of that. Unit
Of space subtracted by one.
It almost rhymes with earth.

What is a poet but a person
Who lives on the ground
Who laughs and listens

Without pretension of knowing
Anything, driven by the lyric's
Quest for rest that never
(God willing) will be found?

Concord, kitchen table, 1966.
Corbetts, Creeley, a grandmother
And me. Sweater, glasses,
One wet eye.

Lots of laughter
Before and after. Every meeting
Rhymed and fluttered into meter.
The beat was the message. . . .

(for Robert Creeley)

13.

Let him become
A great saint
And let me live
To see it.

Let three arrive
And I'll say to all
Give him enough

Room and hemp
To wrap
The children in.

I was who?

The self talks to itself.

Running under
Giving orders to God

Similar selves shudder
In a shadow like mine.

If this is the end of a road
I like its annunciation:

Let him become
A great saint
And his soul
A mother of millions.

14.

My own me was haunted by a shovel
That chased me through the trees.

It called Hurry home to Mummy
And her theater of the drunk

Or "I'll get there first!"

15.

Yes, the Mannings were shop-keepers.
And I am one of them.

Ireland and its cliff-torn charts
Are engraved in my psyche.

Sick around the rich.
Hostile and obsequious.
Communist, Catholic and over-excited.

16.

The potato eaters in my background
Never got to emigrate, only to wait.

Now I ask for the grace to rent and not to keep.
Unemployment, oceans and a drink.

What's in my bag?

A spyglass, a passport, some tickets and a book,
A sandwich and a map of

A village before the eviscerations
Of Marketplace began.

17.

What you learn from torture
Is your physical nature.
Many lives pass before your eyes.

A little ramp down to a river
Before the tides increase the water
On the feast of Our Lady of Carmel.

Two children's foreheads
Before the inhabitation of mind by being.
Yes, God, I baptized them.

18.

In the true idea (Father said)
There is no dying
Because the world is imaginary.

If a flash of green
Foresees our sun as a star
At least you lived among colors.

Adapt to the night
And since the world has already ended
No need to fear your sleep.

19.

"Now then.
Say The Lord's Prayer.
Now then.
I'll leave on a light
And change your sheets
And wash your brush
In the morning.

Now then.
Nestle down.
Night is drawing nigh.
The mourning dove coos.
The hedge is bittersweet
And the violet still blue.

The fuchsia dances
On many legs.
In the bath there's a spider
And in the hall
Some dust.
I'll get a broom
And a hot water bag.

Now then.
Your bed is fresh.
Our Father Who Art In Heaven.
It's 7 pm, Dublin, 1947.
Be patient.

Your time will come."
Love from Grandma Manning.

20.

All activity was religious in sixth-and seventh-century
    Northern India. Cooking, eating, bathing, sleeping.
Even poetry was a form of yoga with self-realization as its goal.
"The whole of speech is Brahman."

Can you separate the gold from the ring?
A cloth of variegated color is like a sentence that is composed
    of different units and now they are one thing.
The color of fluid in a pea-hen's egg becomes the array of
    color in the peacock's spread.

What is uttered aloud by a speaker awakens the sleeper who
    hears.
The two share their understanding and each perceive that the
    same sleeper is speaking between them.
This is consciousness: what is asleep and what is shared.
How is it shared? On the air. Sound cannot exist without air.
    Sound is an attribute of air.

Words end in silence when the sentences have reached perfect
    clarity.
Perfect clarity is also called eternity.
Only at the end can you recognize any meaning.

Why does this matter?
Because the structures of language and sound offer one more
    way to get close to *Atman-Brahman-Ma*.

They reveal secrets by which you can reach enlightenment
    and live in the universe without fear.

21.

Ma is God but not quite the same.
So pray to the toilet, flush.
Pray to the floor, stay clean.
Pray to the quilt, keep me warm tonight.
To the seeds, don't shrivel.
To the cells of the children, fight off infection.
To my hands, work.
To all my perceptions, don't dull.
To my mind, don't forget.
To the cow and the hen, thank you
For all you have given
To us workers of the world.
And to my heartbeat, time me, correctly.
I pray to my pill, give me sleep.
To my wine, stir laughter.
Then I close my eyes and pray to the gray matter:
Leave the light on, Mother.

22.

Kiss the children for me, Ma.
They know why I feed you grain.

An ionic force binds me to your marble.
You swallow whatever I give you.

You accept what is offered and are not discharged into
     forward.
Your body is consecrated in every shade and nail.

Where your energy merges with space it turns light.

You are open to every level—cosmic, intellectual, emotional
    and little.
Physically you assume the shape of ovals.

You liked, in later life to go
Back to the place you left as a child.
You liked to be alone
With very few possessions but a bed.

You just wanted to wander and sit with Maxwell's Demon by
    your side.
Then you could see it was a triumph that nothing worked
    out.

23.

In the milk and meat factory
Where hide and curd are also made, there hangs a heart.

I think it's an udder as puffy and pink as a lady's slipper.
This dark red object is hooked and hard.

Is it real or d—d?

One, I am sure it is made of a cow.
Two, I am sure it represents sacrifice.
But there is no three to what I know.
Because the spirit keeps its distance
From such a place and blows in the lots outside.

Ma knew I was lost.
Both good and evil are capacities
You can access by mistake because the two look alike.
I couldn't decide.
So she made me labor in the factory.

Slaves can't make choices
Therefore they are free.
This is called "the little way."
Every survivor has a slave in their river.
And a section they ran from.

Faces of babies gaze up from under.
It's the population we sense
When we go in the river. Not royalty
Unless one rotten with water
But a slave left over from the will to work.

A person turned into a tool bent to a hard surface.
History glued to spirit every time.

24.

No shoes needed
No bread
No knife and spoon, no glass
No table to work at
No vine for wine
No cushion for the head
No bedding at all
No book, no pen
No cigarette
Nothing round
No prophylactic
No telephone

The radio can go. One last dream
While the life of the brain
Disperses through the cells
Of molecules into the colors it deserves.

—Is it cold out there?
—Will I need a coat?

No coat
No boots
No gloves
No hat
No underwear
No socks

—But silence reminds me of snow and water

No me
No reminds
No shovel
No silence
No igloo
No fire or fur
No plane
No sled
No dog
No fish
No hand

—Well, then I will be free
I will be free from she
She will be freed from me
He will be neither him nor mine

All to colors gone
All music, all birdsong
All words, all sounds,
All to colors gone.

Scrape and Bell

1.

Once I was in bed with the children, it was early in the day
Not even light at eight o'clock in Ireland.
Well, just getting light and we were surrounded by stones
And the Atlantic and the night wind had settled down.
The baby screamed down the hall.
Outside the sea was lashing the backs of the waves with whips.
The curlews still sang.
I was reading *The Secret Garden* so the kids would feel safe
Because the dangers were in another room close by,
Not outside in the rocks, sea and slime,
Not even in the sky except as prophecy.

It was the first AA hour when the priests and police met out
    of uniform.

The night had gone like a thread of logic that can't be sustained.
The shades were pulled down.

Does a thing go somewhere else or disappear?
Music for instance, *The Quartet for the End of Time.*
I will ask a little boy to let me know
When he grows up to be a musician.

The lyric is a form of human thought computing numbers
And how they relate to each other, especially through their
    letters.

Fog and winter light.
Twig-trees, flat fields and an olive tree
Were covered by hay to keep it alive.
Silver and tough evergreen, 15th century walls,
The tragic sand long ago
Absorbed the souls of those who drowned.

We live in a medieval world.
Nothing is real that can't be found.
Many faces in the earth below and sperm in the sea.
This is the promised wilderness.
Who can go nowhere?

From one word to another, the uncreated stays thought.
What can you make of being nowhere?
There is the clunk of the back of the ship going up.
There is the dull buzz of the water below.
Cabin fever, yellow sheets.

The Western person is a mass person.
We can only go inside to hide.

2.

Between Roundstone and Clifden
There lives a priest named Dunleavy who is kind.
He says, "God, grant me the serenity to accept the things
I cannot change, the courage to change the things I can
And the wisdom to know the difference."

In many countries Mass is celebrated
Every two weeks by a priest from a faraway place
Who travels from parish to parish and in between
Someone passes out the consecrated host to those who seek it.

A monk said, "This will increasingly become the case around
    the world,
And suit our nomadic spirit. A new kind of priest will be a
    woman
At home with bread to put into the palms of her neighbors.

She will receive a kit containing the eucharist and a manual.
It will sit in her cupboard with cereal, salt, oil and jam.

In times of natural disaster (famine, war, drought) the woman will pass
Her neighbors a consecrated leaf of grass
With all the usual words of blessing. *Fine. Good. Let it be.*"

3.

The children loved the strangers when they were kind.
Paul held one's hand and Peter called the other Darling.

A Sherman tank was festooned with snow.
Gold snow, pink snow, silver snow, blue snow.

Sex and d—th arrive together everywhere.
Did you know? This is my report.
Experience is ambiguous.

Prayer weak as a worm uncurled on my pillow.
We were all waiting for the pandemic
To hurry things along.

The long way is flat because you take half-steps.
There's a stone at the end or a glove-full of ashes.

4.

A person is an emission.
A jet of light speeding alongside the others.

All of us glowing, our faces twisted
With the effort, shot forward but trying to decide.

Being a bullet with heart would be about the same.
Not a plane full of killers, not a bird.

War comes at you anyway, since people prepare.
An embrace of opposites, how nations
Get to know each other well.

A salacious leap on the women and buildings fall down.
At home the mean men just play war games on airplanes
Or watch sex.

Night drivers in the motel parking lot
Give me the only light I've got.
Without them I would be stuck at the mouth of sleep.

5.

Travelers and immigrants, know your colors.

Eternity is black, infinity is blue, a desert is yellow

And the river is green. Belief is orange.
The horizon is silver.

If something is small, paint it red.
If something is big, make it shine.

If it's a golden memory, the task
Is to turn it back into wheat.

Sheet Music

Night

The night is July, the aura is rain.
The bay is always at low tide.
Green slime covers the sand
Where herons stop, look and listen.
The sand is as thin as clay.

Men in the night
Leave their caravans and run
Across black grass
To the River Argideen
To claim a position for fishing
Like waiting at baggage claim.

The people in the temperance hall
Hold a dance that most of them watch
From their chairs bitterly.
They can see their shoes are history.

The world was remade before they died.

The herons on the Lee
Are slick with slime, fermenting.
Lots of money is exchanged
In the medieval town.
Beer is fomented in silver silos
And no fish swim. One day down
Carpe diem.
No one knows what's coming.

The nuclear weapons programs continue.
A boy in a trap drawn by an elegant horse
Trots through Clonakilty.
Men watch and women shop.
Organic food planted in the middle

Of gourmet olives and jellies.
Thanks and *help*
Are prayer words in fair trade and churches.

Just go in and have a drink at dark.
It's a kind of Sabbath.
In a public house you feel safe with the others.

By now you know the black river has fish
And flowers on it white and shaped
Like strawberry plants.
Two neon kingfishers speed by blue.

Everyone is there for everyone else's fun.
Those men in the night aren't so bad.

A body: this is what it feels
And this is what it feels like.

Sites of massacre and ashes, tin-topped rubble,
Porcelain ovens, jails, a waiting hospital.

Not when it's eternal low tide in a place outside
And birds drain the sand with their appetites.

The Road to Ennis

Near the river Fergus
I saw a beautiful place to live.
I pray to someone living, Maire,
Can I live there?

Two pregnant donkeys in one field.
Five euros found behind a high fence.
Three seals and two pieces of bacon in a bay.
Three flowered beds in one room.

A grain of salt on a child's tongue
To remind her of the soil she came from.
And to which she must return.
Salt is the only rock we eat.

Everything like that
Was on the road to Ennis.
Patch up the cracks in the Catholic church!
It's falling down.

Soon it will be air and stone.
And the stone will be thrown
By a glacial melt
All the way to Rome.

Every minute in vehicle or flesh,
We argued on behalf of sex
And all repressed drives.
Who can adapt to contraptions?

Why are the women rebelling
And perplexed? A priest
Delivered the last cut:
"They are egotists!"

Nowhere is better than a road
To a bog.
Bungalows rot
And bugs drive buyers off.

At Baron's Court

The falling snow will melt before seven
And no one will know.
It lies on the terrace.
Gnarled letters.
Raked bricks. Old roses
Rot in a cap of ice.
No cats, no mice.

This is a light morning snow
That like spittle dribbles
On the stones and fades
Into rivulets.
Green frozen lettuce on the banks.

A Palestinian flag waves
In this small Irish town,
The correspondence being
Children throwing stones.

Behold clouds Irishly low
And silver. Weather is a god
More potent than money
And war. Protean, indifferent,
It will resurrect then crucify
Without mercy.

The south turns into the north
At the border. Structures grow stern
And Norman. The fields
Are beaten into submission
And narrow lipped stone houses
Wonder if there are distinctions
Between humans (worth knowing).

Nowhere is better
Than a road without judgment.

The Question

So why, then, did you leave the village
    Of your childhood?

Why did you opt for a gray and brutalist zone
Devoted to might and money
      Unless you wanted some?
      Why else?
In the airport restaurants you smell shit,
And in the motel fabrics
      Sex and smoke make you gag.

Restless business men, too many of them,
Blink into machines they carry on the planes.

Discarded anti-depressants
Are replaced by vodka and cranberry.

      They call women by their wives' names.
      They have medicinal eyes
      That can't cure anyone.
You go up to 33,000 feet

With an abject army of travelers
Some wear pale army fatigues around the terminals.

When the soldiers see themselves
In plate glass reflections, they are proud
To be protecting this free-for-all.
      Be grateful!
      They *are* heroes!

        Why did you leave the village
        To help support these things
        With your interest?

To what end?
To bury yourself alive among millions!
To suffer work without reward!
>Do you prefer to remember more than to live
>>Inside the limits offered to you at birth?

That village was made of intelligent stones.
>(Stones have brains too.)
Its port was built on a gentle bay
>And among all the swimmers--
>Their penises and eggs and genius--.
>Even the shark
>>(A symbol of the modern world)
>Served a function.
>A fish knows what it is. Even the clouds
Are mindful and the rain burns up thought
Falling from consciousness into all these brains
>Made of the same matter.

Why did you walk out from under the stars
Of your ordinary town?
Why carry your soul the child through dishes
Of hors d'oeuvres (as a waiter), gossip
And even participate in the conversation?
>The shrubs need watering.
>The birds are dry.

The trees are rotting from lack of attention.
>Why didn't you care for them?
>You are too late to analyze
>Or care for the economy and its competitions.
This is the sad part.
You left home in order to find a home.
>You wanted to build it yourself this time.

Why else seek with such fervor
>And uncertainty

The fragments of the familiar?
To think of yourself this way as special?
The only one for the job?

Did you leave in order to track red lights and green
Through the traffic because they looked like Christmas?
To taste the bitter honey on
A stranger's tongue—
To hear him roaring instructions
To people poorer than he—
To be reminded of your teacher?
To see in his cold green eyes
A drop of the sea you played in?
In his hairy chest a replication
Of your father who protected you?
Is that why you went?

Did you leave in order to retrieve
These little bits of experience
And add them to your secret cache?
So you could bring them back
And give a lecture on what you discovered:
That specks of the lost
Can only be identified as "lost."

Why didn't you just stay home?
Once you were a carrier of both child and soul
But when you became a self
You bundled them up
And took them out of the city limits.
You lacked the capacity for carrying so much.

Still, you wanted to rebuild your village
Out of the pieces that shine and remind you
How safe and happy you were on its park benches
On days of no school.
Why did you leave your native country

To become a different kind of being:
    A realist
Who can recognize and classify the pieces of the lost.
    To be the only one!

It's true they sparkle as they vanish
And finding them lets you know you are credible,
    At home in the world.

The Abbey

The Shannon River
Is erased by fog like white flowers
Perpetuating the best honey.

Meantime the chirp of the birds is the flower-making sound.

The next parish
Over is Boston or Newfoundland, depending
Where you turn your craft.

Water in its massive restraints remains
A wilderness.

There are no crickets
Here anymore, no butterflies to instruct
Flowers how to fly.

Knocks, bangs
And shoveling go on from eight to four,

The scrape and bell of the tossed shovel
On concrete. Matins is never late.

The men who prefer to be with men sing
While the ones who like a woman at home
Labor with machines.

My cell
Is an aggregate in a sequence.

Wasps and bees tick on the glass.
I have already made a mess.
They are building buildings, a new gift shop
And entrance to the refectory.

My window faces the top tier of stained glass
In the massive concrete church.

A liminal disquiet, like time
Turning spirited outside in the hall.

I have been dispatched to become fretless
And transparent, someone needing no one.

Flanked by monks my fear of men recedes.
But I am just a guest, a woman of the road.

A guest should feel at home
The way a drinker becomes a thinker
When he is at his least coherent.

A guest must never outlive her welcome.
Die, or leave—before they want you gone.
A guest can only guess
What is really going on.
The walls have no ears, the toilets are like megaphones.

The kitchen is alien
And everyone who lives there is giving her
Anything she needs, there is no question
Of meanness, but a guest must leave her host
In order to remain a guest.

No Sleep

Now my nests are empty or rotting.
Now old skulls moonlight in their holes.
Now is the time of the spirit.
Tonight, this hour and minute.

Find a shell or a flute, inhabit it with music.

No ways open for a mind.
No ways for the inexistent.
The fruit tree is pinned to a wall so the fruits
Are less likely to fall.

Fall they will. Clouds are on the ground
Rain across a swan
Water stopped by stone
Rebellious bushes
Flowers storm
The whitethorn alone
With a horse
Coole Park a dungeon
Of leaves and black holes
Soggy corridors
No sons, no daughters
No poets, no more house.

Fanny Howe is a poet, novelist, essayist, and translator. She is the author of over twenty-five books, including *Selected Poems*, which won the 2001 Lenore Marshall Poetry Prize. She currently lives in New England.

The Lyrics has been typeset using Trump Mediaeval, a typeface designed by Georg Trump and first issued in 1954 by the Weber Foundry, Stuttgart, Germany. Book design by Wendy Holdman. Composition at Prism Publishing Center, Minneapolis, Minnesota. Manufactured by Bang Printing on acid-free paper.